AFFIRSLAYTIONS

Affirmations to Slay Your Day the SUGARBAKER way

AffirSLAYtions: Affirmations to Slay Your Day the Sugarbaker Way
ISBN 978-1-960326-78-2
Copyright © 2024 by Miss Terra Cotta Sugarbaker

All rights reserved. No part of this book may be reproduced or transmitted in any form or by any means, electronic or mechanical, including photocopying, recording, or by any information storage and retrieval system, without permission in writing from the publisher.

Tehom Center Publishing is a 501c3 non-profit imprint of Parson's Porch Books. Tehom Center Publishing celebrates feminist and queer authors, with a commitment that at least half our authors are people of color. Its face and voice is Rev. Dr. Angela Yarber.

DEDICATION:

For Kevin, my manager, my guard, my love.

For Jon Santos, my fairy godmother, and Claudia Strange, who believed that the world needed more literate drag.

For Stacy, who loved me from day one.

For Angela, who knew I had a story to tell.

For all of the librarians creating safety in the stacks.

Miss Terra Cotta Sugarbaker is the revolutionary drag queen behind Atlanta's first Drag story hour. Believing reading is truly fundamental, she has created safe spaces for children and the young at heart. Here are her tips for a fab life. Apply these affirmations to slay your day the Sugarbaker way!

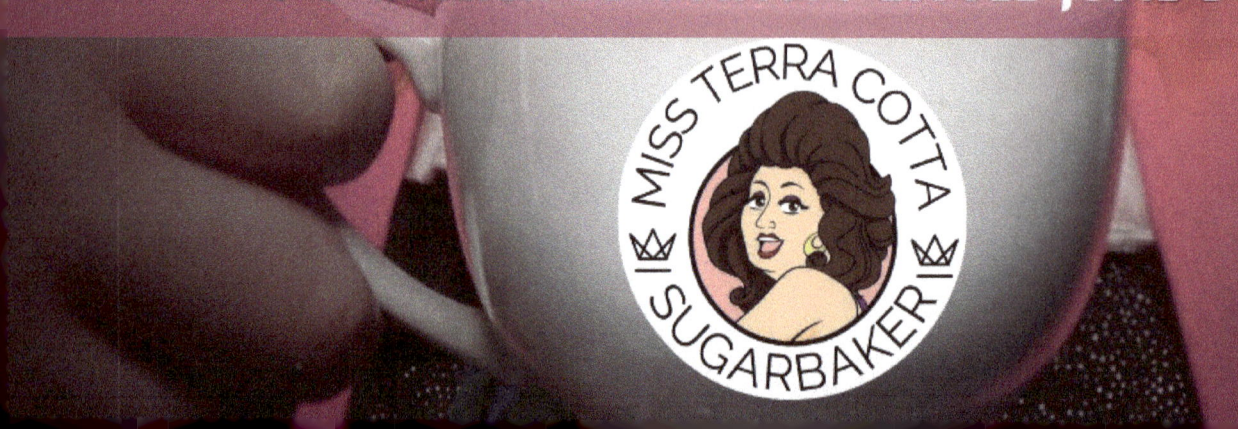

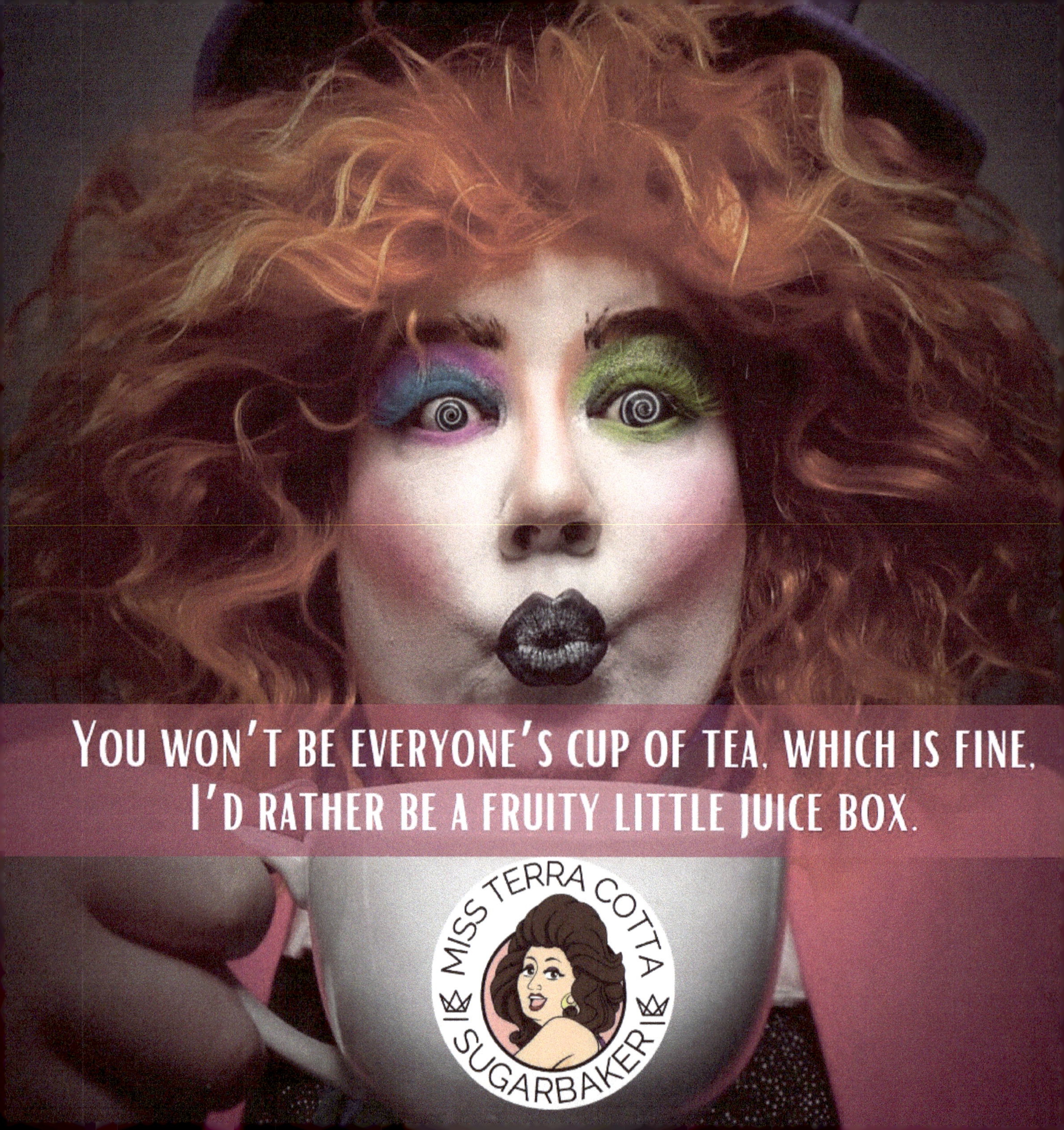
YOU WON'T BE EVERYONE'S CUP OF TEA, WHICH IS FINE,
I'D RATHER BE A FRUITY LITTLE JUICE BOX.
MISS TERRA COTTA
SUGARBAKER

Like the library, I am full of mystery, comedy, drama and romance.

I am worthy of all the space I occupy in this world.